PIONEERS

By Mabel Harmer
Pictures by Loran Wilford

A most dramatic chapter in our country's story was written in courage by the pioneers.

They packed their wagons, hitched up the oxen, and left the security of their eastern homes to cross mountains without roads and rivers without bridges. They built homes in the wilderness in the face of dangers.

This is a straight account, for young readers, of where the pioneers came from, how they traveled, the dangers they overcame, the homes they built, and how they lived in them.

The "true book" series is prepared
under the direction of
Illa Podendorf
Laboratory School, University of Chicago
Ninety-eight per cent of the text is in words from
the Combined Word List for Primary Reading

the true book of

PIONEERS

By Mabel Harmer

Illustrations by Loran Wilford

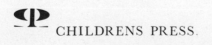 CHILDRENS PRESS.

TABLE OF

F

CONTENTS

WHERE PIONEERS CAME FROM

About a hundred and fifty years after the pilgrims settled in this country, a young hunter picked up his gun. He tossed it onto his shoulder and followed a buffalo trail across the mountains into what is now Kentucky.

His name was Daniel Boone.

He found wild country. There were
no settlers, no roads. Indians
hunted in the woods for food. The
country was beautiful and dangerous.
But here was rich, free land — miles
and miles of it.

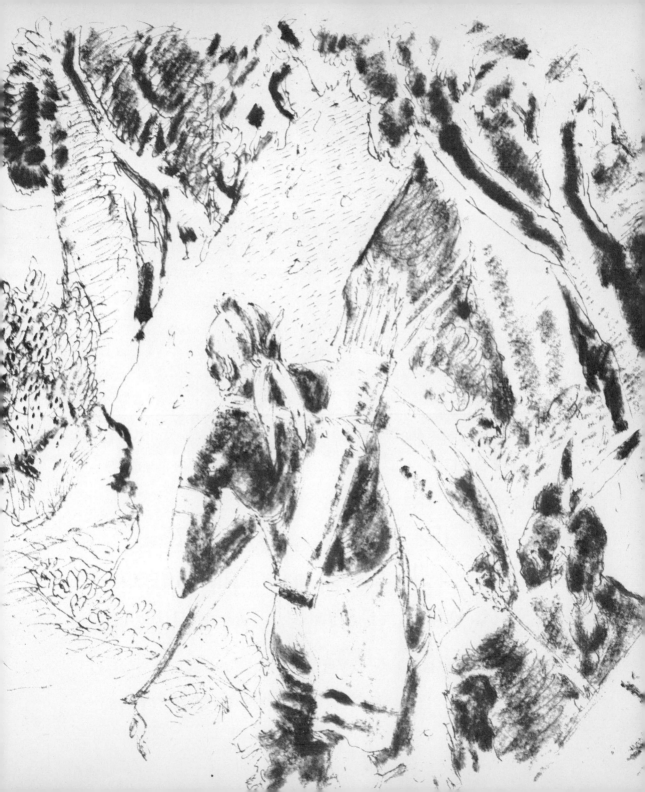

Many settlers, besides the Pilgrims,
had come to the shores of America.
But they had stayed on the safe land
between the sea and the mountains.

Now there were big, beautiful farms
like George Washington's *Mount
Vernon*. There were small farms, too.
Busy young cities were called *Boston,
New York, Philadelphia.*

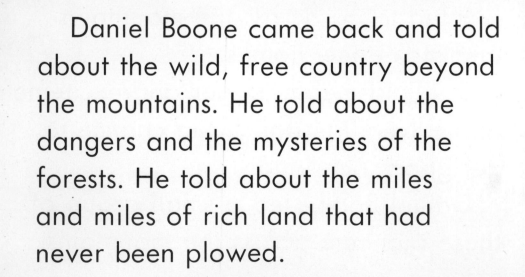

Daniel Boone came back and told
about the wild, free country beyond
the mountains. He told about the
dangers and the mysteries of the
forests. He told about the miles
and miles of rich land that had
never been plowed.

N.H.

BOSTON

MASS.

CONN. R.I.

NEW YORK

N. JERSEY

Atlantic

PHILADELPHIA

MARYLAND

VIRGINIA

Ocean

NORTH CAROLINA

S.C

GA

People listened. A few of them wanted to go across the mountains and make new homes.

It would mean danger and excitement and adventure, and a big chance to get good, rich land.

Daniel Boone led a small group of these pioneers across the mountains.

Fur traders, men searching for gold, and hunters, like Daniel Boone, had seen this wild country west of the mountains. But the American pioneers were the first to go and build their homes in the new land.

A pioneer is one who goes first and opens the way for others to follow.

There were no roads.

There were rivers with no bridges.

There were Indians and wild animals in the woods.

For a hundred years, after Daniel Boone showed a way across the mountains, American pioneers moved westward toward the other ocean.

Their exciting story is part of the history of our country.

HOW THEY TRAVELED

Some pioneers traveled on foot.
Some rode horses or mules.
But most of the families used
covered wagons.

Wagon wheels were wide for rolling
through soft earth.

Wagon ends were high, so that
things would not slide out on the hills.
They were loaded with flour,
salt, cornmeal, bedding, tools, a
few pieces of furniture. There
would be no stores where they were
going.

Most of the wagons were pulled
by oxen. Oxen were slow, but they
were strong.

Sometimes trees had to be cut
down to clear a path. A wagon wheel
would hit a rock and break.

Heavy rains made great mud holes.
Uphill travel was hard, and down-
hill travel was dangerous. Strong
men tied ropes to the wagon and
hung on to keep it from going down,
end over end.

There were times when the pioneers
could move down a river on a flatboat.
No matter how they traveled, they
could go only a few miles in a day.

DANGERS ON THE WAY

The oxen could pull the wagons across small streams. But there were deep rivers to cross, too.

Logs were tied to the wheels to keep the wagons afloat.

The oxen swam and pulled the wagons across.

Men on swimming horses helped to guide them.

Sometimes a wagon broke loose and swung away and upset.

Herds of buffalo on the plains
could be dangerous.

Great numbers of them, thundering
along could destroy everything in
their path.

Indians were not always friendly.
There was real danger from Indians.
Often several wagons traveled
together in a "wagon train."

At night the wagons were pulled
into a circle and the oxen were
kept in the center.

Pioneers could protect themselves
better this way, and keep the animals
out of the reach of the Indians.

Within the circle, the women
cooked. The children played or
danced to fiddle music.

There were many dangers but the
pioneers bravely faced them. There
was fun and adventure, too.

PIONEER HOMES

The first thing the pioneer did at the end of his journey was to build a small house.

Logs from trees on the land were cut to fit together for the walls and the chimney. The cracks were filled with mud. If there were no trees, homes were built of sod, blocks of earth held together with grass roots.

The first house, usually, had just one room with a dirt floor.

If there were neighbors, they came and helped build the house. The women brought food.

They danced and sang to fiddle music when the house was finished.

Pioneers had to make play of their hard work.

Beds had deerskin strips or ropes laced back and forth to make the springs.

Mattresses were filled with straw or cattails. Few pioneer women had feathers for their mattresses.

Sometimes there was a "trundle bed" which was pushed under the big bed during the day. Sometimes there was a wooden cradle.

A table was made of thick boards on posts. Chairs had rawhide seats.

Soap was made over a fire outside. Water with lye and fat in it was boiled for hours. When a spoonful was firm and white, the soap was done. It was poured into a tub to cool and was then cut into bars.

Candles were used for light.

These were made by pouring deer or sheep fat into molds with wicks strung through them.

The spinning wheel and loom had an important place in a pioneer home.

The heart of the home was the fireplace where the cooking was done in iron kettles that swung over the fire.

Tubs, churns, and some dishes were made of wood.

FOOD AND CLOTHING

The men and boys of pioneer families would hunt and fish for fresh meat.

The girls could find greens and berries in the woods.

Vegetables and fruits were raised in a garden. These were stored in a dirt cellar for winter use. Or dried and hung from the ceiling of the cabin.

The women made their own butter and cheese.

As the land was cleared, corn was raised and ground into meal. Hulls were soaked off to make hominy.

Pioneers had little sugar. They
got honey when they could find a tree
with bees in it — a bee-tree.

If there were sugar-maple trees
near by, they collected the sap
and boiled it into syrup and sugar.

Deerskin was sometimes used for clothing.

Cloth had to be made at home. Sheep's wool, when they had sheep, was spun into thread and woven into cloth on a loom.

Stockings, caps, mittens, scarves were knitted.

Flax and cotton were sometimes raised and used to make summer clothes.

Pioneer women made their own colors for dyeing cloth.

Green was made from sage brush and alum.

Brown was made from peach leaves or walnuts.

Purple and red were made from madder berries.

Yellow was made from rabbit brush.

Shoes were hard to make.

Hides of deer, sheep and cattle were used. These had to be soaked in salt water with tree bark for months to soften them. Wooden pegs were sometimes used to fasten the soles to the shoes.

Later, when there were more pioneer homes, a shoemaker would come by with his tools and make shoes for a whole family.

PIONEER CHILDREN

Pioneer children had very few toys except some homemade ones.

But a boy learned to handle a gun and to bring home a rabbit or a squirrel for dinner.

A girl might have a rag doll, but she also learned to spin and weave and knit and churn the butter.

A boy brought in wood for the fire and water for cooking.

Work was part of the lives of the children, but they learned the ways of the woods and made pets of some of the baby animals.

At night there was corn to pop in
the fire. And songs and stories
were important. A Bible was often
the only book, and from it the
children learned to read.

The gayest times of all were when neighbors came to help make a quilt or husk the corn. These work parties were called "bees."

The children played games and joined in the dancing in the evening.

Pioneer children did not often have a school to go to. If they did, it was a one-room cabin where they learned from what books they could bring from home. They wrote on slates with a slate pencil, or on smooth wooden paddles with a piece of charcoal.

In summer, the children took a
long bar of homemade soap and
bathed in the creek.

HOW NEWS TRAVELED

One of the greatest hardships for
the pioneers was that there was
almost no way of getting news
and mail.

About ninety-two years went by
after Daniel Boone led a small group
of pioneers over the mountains. Many
settlers had built homes in the
wide stretch of the country.

Towns grew where several families
settled in one place. Roads were
better, but not good.

The railroad, the "Iron Horse,"
had crept across the country as far
as the Missouri River. It brought

news and mail from the East.

About this time the Pony Express carried mail from St. Joseph, Missouri, to Sacramento, California. Fresh, fast ponies were picked up at relay stations, and the 2000 miles were covered in 10 days.

Stagecoaches made regular runs between towns.

THE GOLDEN SPIKE

Within another eight years, the railroad crossed the whole, wide country.

The track coming from the East met the one coming from the West.

A golden spike was driven to celebrate. The first chain of railroads crossed the whole American continent.

This brought towns in the East and the West within a week's journey of each other. It opened up new lands for settlement. Dangerous journeys cross-country in covered wagons were no longer necessary.

About a hundred years had gone by since Daniel Boone came over the mountains with that small group of settlers. The pioneers had opened up the way and this country grew to what it is today.

E73-15204   F 2ND

HARMER, MABEL
 THE TRUE BOOK OF PIONEERS.